NEW MATH

EQUATIONS FOR LIVING

CRAIG DAMRAUER

**Andrews McMeel
Publishing, LLC**

Kansas City

Printed in China.

No part of this book may be used or reproduced in any manner whatsoever without written permission except in the case of reprints in the context of reviews. For information, write Andrews McMeel Publishing, LLC, an Andrews McMeel Universal company, 4520 Main Street, Kansas City, Missouri 64111.

 A Quirk Packaging Book

ISBN-13: 978-0-7407-6057-0
ISBN-10: 0-7407-6057-2

Library of Congress Control Number: 2006922718

06 07 08 09 10 OGP 10 9 8 7 6 5 4 3 2 1

www.andrewsmcmeel.com

ATTENTION: SCHOOLS AND BUSINESSES
Andrews McMeel books are available at quantity discounts with bulk purchase for educational, business, or sales promotional use. For information, please write to: Special Sales Department, Andrews McMeel Publishing, LLC, 4520 Main Street, Kansas City, Missouri 64111.

With much love for my wife, Desiree Andrepont,
and our great friend, Missy Wilson.
You both, in your own special ways, made this book possible.

CLEANLINESS =

GODLINESS – 1

BEAUTY =

PUBLIC OPINION + THE EYE OF THE BEHOLDER

REVENGE =

DO UNTO OTHERS — AS YOU WOULD HAVE THEM DO UNTO YOU

COMPASSION =

$$\frac{\text{WHAT IF THAT WERE ME?}}{\text{I'M GLAD THAT'S NOT ME}}$$

ANGER =

TICKED OFF³

MATURITY =

THINGS YOU
USED TO DO — THINGS YOU
USED TO DO

IGNORANCE =

$$\frac{\text{IT}}{\text{WHAT I KNOW ABOUT IT}}$$

HAPPY =

UNHAPPY — UN

SANITY =

$$\frac{\text{EVERYONE ELSE'S CRAZINESS}}{\text{MINE}}$$

CRAZY =

TALKING TO ONESELF $-$ (CELL PHONE $+$ EAR PIECE)

INSOMNIA =

1:51 A.M. + ETERNITY + 1:52 A.M. + ETERNITY + 1:53 A.M. + ETERNITY

CLAUSTROPHOBIA =

$$\frac{YOU}{SPACE}$$

UNIQUENESS =

UNIQUENESS

DISAPPOINTMENT =

EXPECTATION

REALITY

BRUNCH =

BREAKFAST + LUNCH + CANTALOUPE

LUNCH =

$$\frac{\text{DINNER}}{1.5} - \text{SWEETS}$$

TV DINNER =

$$\frac{\text{THE FOUR FOOD GROUPS}}{4} + \text{DESSERT}$$

ONIONS =

WEEPING – CATHARSIS

RAISIN =

GRAPE + TIME

SWEET TOOTH =

$$\frac{\text{TASTE}}{\text{NUTRITION}}$$

BACKYARD =

MANIFEST DESTINY + FENCES

FENCES =

$$\frac{\text{WHAT THE NEIGHBORS THINK}}{\text{WHAT THEY KNOW}}$$

DOGGIE DAY CARE =

KENNEL — GUILT

DOG =

CAT + LOYALTY

GOOD DOG =

$$\frac{\text{BARK}}{\text{BITE}}$$

BAD DOG =

$$\frac{\text{BITE}}{\text{BARK}}$$

STANDARD POODLE =

POODLE — EMBARRASSMENT

RAT =

(MOUSE x 4) – CUTE

LOVE =

LIKE x LIKE

MAYBE =

$$\frac{YES}{NO} + \frac{NO}{YES}$$

MARRIAGE =

**TILL DEATH
DO US PART** — DIVORCE

PATERNITY =

WHAT? + ARE YOU SURE?

NAGGING =

SAFETY =

WHAT WOULD YOUR MOM SAY?

IGNORE YOUR MOM

GRANDMA =

$$\frac{\text{WISDOM}}{\text{BATTINESS}}$$

DEADBEAT DAD =

PATERNITY

RESPONSIBILITY

UNCLE =

DAD + FUN

MIDLIFE CRISIS =

$$\frac{\text{WHAT I WANT TO DO}}{\text{WHAT I'VE DONE}} \pm \text{FAST CAR}$$

NIHILISM =

$$\frac{\text{EXISTENCE}}{\text{EXISTENCE}} \times 0$$

JUNIOR HIGH SCHOOL =

JAIL + PUBERTY

TEEN ANGST =

HORMONES

PHILOSOPHY

PARALLEL PARKING =

BUMPER CARS _ AMUSEMENT PARK

SPEED BUMP =

SLOW DOWN + TOO LATE

ESCALATOR =

STAIRS — THIGH MUSCLES

CREDIT CARD =

I CAN'T — I CAN'T
AFFORD IT   AFFORD IT

INFOMERCIAL =

INFORMATION + COMMERCIAL + BUT WAIT, THERE'S MORE

HOLLYWOOD =

$$\frac{\text{FLASH}}{\text{SUBSTANCE}} + \text{DAMN FINE WEATHER}$$

PREQUEL =

SEQUEL – 2

RUMOR =

$$\frac{DISTANCE}{TRUTH}$$

SHOCK =

EXPECTATION — EXPECTATION

COLLATERAL DAMAGE =

KILLING – THE DEATH PART

TRUTH =

$$\frac{\text{WHAT I THINK HAPPENED}}{\text{WHAT REALLY HAPPENED}}$$

BULLY =

A JERK — 1 GOOD ASS KICKING

INTERNSHIP =

SHITWORK + COLLEGE CREDIT

OFFICE WORKERS =

ANTS — 4 LEGS — 2 FEELERS

FILING =

PAPER – ENTROPY

GOOD MEETING =

$$\frac{\text{TIME SAVED}}{\text{TIME WASTED}} + \text{SNACKS}$$

BAD MEETING =

$$\frac{\text{TIME WASTED}}{\text{TIME SAVED}} + \text{SNACKS}$$

OFFICE COFFEE =

(COFFEE — GOOD) + UNWANTED CHITCHAT

DRUNK =

FREEDOM OF SPEECH + SLURRING

SANTA CLAUS =

THE TOOTH FAIRY + 250 LBS

TRICK OR TREAT =

EXTORTION + OH, ISN'T THAT CUTE?

MIME =

JUGGLER – BALLS

PING-PONG =

$$\frac{\text{TENNIS}}{8} + \text{LOOKING FOR THE BALL UNDER THE SOFA}$$

HANDBALL =

RACQUETBALL — RACKET

CAMPING =

WHAT'S THAT SOUND? +
DO YOU THINK IT'S A BEAR?
+ THERE'S A ROCK IN THE
SMALL OF MY BACK + THAT
DEFINITELY SOUNDS LIKE
A BEAR + HOW'D YOU SLEEP?
+ NEVER BETTER

THE WEATHER FORECAST =

PARTLY RIGHT + PARTLY WRONG ± 50%

UMBRELLA =

RAIN − WET + A SHARP STICK IN THE EYE

SILENCE =

CAR ALARM =

THE BOY
WHO CRIED + AMPLIFICATION
WOLF

CARJACKING =

CAN I BORROW YOUR CAR? — NO, YOU CAN'T

ENTRAPMENT =

YOU'RE GONNA
DO IT ANYWAY   + COPS

MILITARY COUP =

RECALL — THE ELECTION

BARBED WIRE =

THE GRASS
IS ALWAYS — VERIFICATION
GREENER

ARTHRITIS =

YOUR HANDS + THE WEATHER FORECAST

MORALITY =

$$\frac{\text{COMPASSION}}{\text{KARMIC RETRIBUTION}}$$

LUXURY =

WEALTH + PILLOWS

MODERN ART =

I COULD
DO THAT + YEAH, BUT
YOU DIDN'T

YOGA =

AEROBICS + 10 YEARS − HEADBANDS

PLASTIC SURGERY =

YOUR BODY — (GRAVITY + TIME)

ECCENTRIC =

CRAZY + WEALTH

VALUE =

PERCEPTION x TIME

LIFE INSURANCE =

GOD
FORBID + JACKPOT!

FIRST IMPRESSION =

EVERYTHING YOU FIGURE OUT LATER — LATER

HINDSIGHT =

COULDA + SHOULDA + WOULDA

DEATH =

NAP + FOREVER

ABOUT THE BOOK

I wrote the first New Math equations for a solo show of my work at Move Lab in Manhattan's Meatpacking District. Eventually, the collection grew into this book. A lot of people have given me their two cents about whether I got these equations right, as well as whether I'm sane or not. My mom suggested I let you do the same. If you'd like to share your own equations or give me some feedback on mine, visit MoreNewMath.com.

ABOUT THE AUTHOR

Craig Damrauer is a writer and artist whose work plays with the abbreviated ways of seeing that are typical of modern culture. He lives in Brooklyn, New York, with his wife and two kids.